Be a student of your own life, your own future, your own destiny.

Take the time to write notes and to keep a journal. You'll be so glad you did.

What a treasure to leave behind when you go.

What a treasure to enjoy today!

-Jim Rohn-

CONTENTS

Guided Journal
For Personal Growth

With Inspirational Quotes
From Jim Rohn

PLE Publishing & Promotions

Journal writing is one of the greatest indications that you're a serious student.

-Jim Rohn-

Be A Student Of Your Own Life

Take a few moments each day to record those important experiences in life to help you grow, live life to the fullest, and become your best self.

Guided 12-Week Personal Growth Journal

Daily guided journal pages help you **GROW** each day by focusing on:

GRATITUDE
Reflections of gratitude by listing at least 3 things for which you are thankful.

REMEMBER
Moments that brought you joy and are worth remembering as part of your life story.

OPPORTUNITIES TO LEARN
Teaching moments from the *University of Life* that provided you with the opportunity to learn and become a better you.

WINS
Moments of personal wins that made you feel successful and fulfilled.

Also, capture experiences and insights with your Daily Reflection pages.

Daily, Weekly, and Monthly Reflections

This 12-week personal growth journal will help you grow by becoming a student of your own life with:

- 12 weeks of daily guided journaling pages.
- Daily blank-lined journaling pages for free-form reflection.
- Inspirational quotes by Jim Rohn throughout the journal.
- Weekly reflection pages to review the past week's lessons, successes, challenges, and important insights.
- Reflection pages every four weeks to review the past month's lessons, successes, challenges, and insights.

Begin your journey of personal growth today!

You cannot change the seasons,
but you can change yourself.
Therein lies the opportunity to
live an extraordinary life.

-Jim Rohn-

Looking Ahead To The Next 4 Weeks

Think about and write down your goals for the coming weeks

What do I want to achieve in the next 4 weeks?

_____

_____

_____

_____

What do I need to accomplish each week to achieve these goals?

Week 1: _____

_____

Week 2: _____

_____

Week 3: _____

_____

Week 4: _____

_____

What habits do I need to develop or reinforce?

_____   _____

_____   _____

_____   _____

What habits must I remove & replace with the above habits?

_____   _____

_____   _____

_____   _____

Week 1

Journaling

Date: 20 / 1 / 22   M T W (TH) F S SU

GRATITUDE - Today I am grateful for:

All the things I have achieved
in my 20's. Especially Lucy and
the kids. They have all grown
into Beautiful people both on
the inside and the Outside.

REMEMBER – A good memory I will cherish from today is:

The kids running into my bedroom
with presents, desperate for
me to open them up.

(True Wealth) Rho Voldas bringing over
a book for my Birthday.

OPPORTUNITIES **T**O **L**EARN - Today I learned that:

Today I learnt about Book
Publishers and how to go
about getting a book published

WINS – Today I accomplished or was successful at:

Today I started my day at the
Gym. The endorphins were a
great way to start the day.

4

Daily Reflection

Date: ___ / ___ / _____   M T W TH F S SU

GRATITUDE - Today I am grateful for:

_____
_____
_____
_____
_____

REMEMBER – A good memory I will cherish from today is:

_____
_____
_____
_____
_____

OPPORTUNITIES TO LEARN - Today I learned that:

_____
_____
_____
_____
_____

WINS – Today I accomplished or was successful at:

_____
_____
_____
_____
_____

Daily Reflection

Date: ___/___/_____   M T W TH F S SU

GRATITUDE - Today I am grateful for:

_____
_____
_____
_____
_____

REMEMBER – A good memory I will cherish from today is:

_____
_____
_____
_____
_____

OPPORTUNITIES **T**O **L**EARN - Today I learned that:

_____
_____
_____
_____
_____

WINS – Today I accomplished or was successful at:

_____
_____
_____
_____
_____

Daily Reflection

Date: ___ / ___ / _____   M T W TH F S SU

GRATITUDE - Today I am grateful for:

_____
_____
_____
_____
_____

REMEMBER – A good memory I will cherish from today is:

_____
_____
_____
_____
_____

OPPORTUNITIES TO LEARN - Today I learned that:

_____
_____
_____
_____
_____

WINS – Today I accomplished or was successful at:

_____
_____
_____
_____
_____

Daily Reflection

Date: ___/___/_____   M T W TH F S SU

GRATITUDE - Today I am grateful for:

_____

_____

_____

_____

_____

REMEMBER – A good memory I will cherish from today is:

_____

_____

_____

_____

_____

OPPORTUNITIES TO LEARN - Today I learned that:

_____

_____

_____

_____

_____

WINS – Today I accomplished or was successful at:

_____

_____

_____

_____

_____

Daily Reflection

Date: ____ / ____ / ____   M T W TH F S SU

GRATITUDE - Today I am grateful for:

_____
_____
_____
_____
_____

REMEMBER – A good memory I will cherish from today is:

_____
_____
_____
_____
_____

OPPORTUNITIES **T**O **L**EARN - Today I learned that:

_____
_____
_____
_____
_____

WINS – Today I accomplished or was successful at:

_____
_____
_____
_____
_____

Daily Reflection

Date: ___ / ___ / ___   M T W TH F S SU

GRATITUDE - Today I am grateful for:

_____

_____

_____

_____

_____

REMEMBER – A good memory I will cherish from today is:

_____

_____

_____

_____

_____

OPPORTUNITIES TO LEARN - Today I learned that:

_____

_____

_____

_____

_____

WINS – Today I accomplished or was successful at:

_____

_____

_____

_____

_____

Daily Reflection

Week 1 Reflection – Looking Back

Take time to reflect on the previous week

GENERAL REFLECTION:
How am I feeling overall about this past week?

_____

_____

_____

_____

_____

_____

CHALLENGES:
What were my greatest challenges this week?

_____

_____

_____

_____

_____

_____

ACHIEVEMENTS:
What were my greatest achievements this week?

_____

_____

_____

_____

_____

_____

Week 1 Reflection – Looking Ahead

Think about my goals and intensions for the coming week

IMPROVEMENT PLAN:
What can I do different this week to become a better person?

_____

_____

_____

_____

_____

_____

GOALS AND PLANS FOR THE COMING WEEK:
What do you want to accomplish this week?

_____

_____

_____

_____

_____

_____

TOP PRIORITY:
What are my top priorities for the coming week?

_____

_____

_____

_____

_____

_____

The major value in life is not what you get. The major value in life is what you become.

-Jim Rohn-

Week 2
Journaling

Date: ___ / ___ / ___   M T W TH F S SU

GRATITUDE - Today I am grateful for:

_____
_____
_____
_____
_____

REMEMBER – A good memory I will cherish from today is:

_____
_____
_____
_____
_____

OPPORTUNITIES TO LEARN - Today I learned that:

_____
_____
_____
_____
_____

WINS – Today I accomplished or was successful at:

_____
_____
_____
_____
_____

Daily Reflection

Date: ___/___/_____   M T W TH F S SU

GRATITUDE - Today I am grateful for:

_____
_____
_____
_____
_____

REMEMBER – A good memory I will cherish from today is:

_____
_____
_____
_____
_____

OPPORTUNITIES **T**O **L**EARN - Today I learned that:

_____
_____
_____
_____
_____

WINS – Today I accomplished or was successful at:

_____
_____
_____
_____
_____

Daily Reflection

Date: ___ / ___ / _____   M T W TH F S SU

GRATITUDE - Today I am grateful for:

_____

_____

_____

_____

_____

REMEMBER – A good memory I will cherish from today is:

_____

_____

_____

_____

_____

OPPORTUNITIES TO LEARN - Today I learned that:

_____

_____

_____

_____

_____

WINS – Today I accomplished or was successful at:

_____

_____

_____

_____

_____

Daily Reflection

Date: ___ / ___ / ___   M T W TH F S SU

GRATITUDE - Today I am grateful for:

_____

_____

_____

_____

_____

REMEMBER – A good memory I will cherish from today is:

_____

_____

_____

_____

_____

OPPORTUNITIES TO LEARN - Today I learned that:

_____

_____

_____

_____

_____

WINS – Today I accomplished or was successful at:

_____

_____

_____

_____

_____

Daily Reflection

Date: ___ / ___ / ___   M T W TH F S SU

GRATITUDE - Today I am grateful for:

_____
_____
_____
_____
_____

REMEMBER – A good memory I will cherish from today is:

_____
_____
_____
_____
_____

OPPORTUNITIES TO LEARN - Today I learned that:

_____
_____
_____
_____
_____

WINS – Today I accomplished or was successful at:

_____
_____
_____
_____
_____

Daily Reflection

Date: ___ / ___ / _____   M T W TH F S SU

GRATITUDE - Today I am grateful for:

_____
_____
_____
_____
_____

REMEMBER – A good memory I will cherish from today is:

_____
_____
_____
_____
_____

OPPORTUNITIES **T**O **L**EARN - Today I learned that:

_____
_____
_____
_____
_____

WINS – Today I accomplished or was successful at:

_____
_____
_____
_____
_____

Daily Reflection

Date: ___ / ___ / _____   M T W TH F S SU

GRATITUDE - Today I am grateful for:

_____
_____
_____
_____
_____

REMEMBER – A good memory I will cherish from today is:

_____
_____
_____
_____
_____

OPPORTUNITIES TO LEARN - Today I learned that:

_____
_____
_____
_____
_____

WINS – Today I accomplished or was successful at:

_____
_____
_____
_____
_____

Daily Reflection

Week 2 Reflection – Looking Back

Take time to reflect on the previous week

GENERAL REFLECTION:
How am I feeling overall about this past week?

_____

_____

_____

_____

_____

_____

_____

CHALLENGES:
What were my greatest challenges this week?

_____

_____

_____

_____

_____

_____

ACHIEVEMENTS:
What were my greatest achievements this week?

_____

_____

_____

_____

_____

_____

Week 2 Reflection – Looking Ahead

Think about my goals and intensions for the coming week

IMPROVEMENT PLAN:
What can I do different this week to become a better person?

_____

_____

_____

_____

_____

_____

GOALS AND PLANS FOR THE COMING WEEK:
What do you want to accomplish this week?

_____

_____

_____

_____

_____

TOP PRIORITY:
What are my top priorities for the coming week?

_____

_____

_____

_____

_____

If you don't design your own life plan, chances are you'll fall into someone else's plan. And guess what they have planned for you? Not much.

-Jim Rohn-

Week 3

Journaling

Date: ___ / ___ / ___   M T W TH F S SU

GRATITUDE - Today I am grateful for:

_____
_____
_____
_____
_____

REMEMBER – A good memory I will cherish from today is:

_____
_____
_____
_____
_____

OPPORTUNITIES TO LEARN - Today I learned that:

_____
_____
_____
_____
_____

WINS – Today I accomplished or was successful at:

_____
_____
_____
_____
_____

Daily Reflection

Date: ___ / ___ / ___   M T W TH F S SU

GRATITUDE - Today I am grateful for:

_____

_____

_____

_____

_____

REMEMBER – A good memory I will cherish from today is:

_____

_____

_____

_____

_____

OPPORTUNITIES TO LEARN - Today I learned that:

_____

_____

_____

_____

_____

WINS – Today I accomplished or was successful at:

_____

_____

_____

_____

_____

Daily Reflection

Date: ___ / ___ / _____   M T W TH F S SU

GRATITUDE - Today I am grateful for:

_____

_____

_____

_____

_____

REMEMBER – A good memory I will cherish from today is:

_____

_____

_____

_____

_____

OPPORTUNITIES **T**O **L**EARN - Today I learned that:

_____

_____

_____

_____

_____

WINS – Today I accomplished or was successful at:

_____

_____

_____

_____

_____

Daily Reflection

Date: ___ / ___ / _____   M T W TH F S SU

GRATITUDE - Today I am grateful for:

_____
_____
_____
_____
_____

REMEMBER – A good memory I will cherish from today is:

_____
_____
_____
_____
_____

OPPORTUNITIES TO LEARN - Today I learned that:

_____
_____
_____
_____
_____

WINS – Today I accomplished or was successful at:

_____
_____
_____
_____
_____

Daily Reflection

Date: ___ / ___ / _____   M T W TH F S SU

GRATITUDE - Today I am grateful for:

_____

_____

_____

_____

_____

REMEMBER – A good memory I will cherish from today is:

_____

_____

_____

_____

_____

OPPORTUNITIES TO LEARN - Today I learned that:

_____

_____

_____

_____

_____

WINS – Today I accomplished or was successful at:

_____

_____

_____

_____

_____

Daily Reflection

Date: ___/___/___   M T W TH F S SU

GRATITUDE - Today I am grateful for:

_____
_____
_____
_____
_____

REMEMBER – A good memory I will cherish from today is:

_____
_____
_____
_____
_____

OPPORTUNITIES **T**O **L**EARN - Today I learned that:

_____
_____
_____
_____
_____

WINS – Today I accomplished or was successful at:

_____
_____
_____
_____
_____

Daily Reflection

Date: ___ / ___ / _____   M T W TH F S SU

GRATITUDE - Today I am grateful for:

_____
_____
_____
_____
_____

REMEMBER – A good memory I will cherish from today is:

_____
_____
_____
_____
_____

OPPORTUNITIES TO LEARN - Today I learned that:

_____
_____
_____
_____
_____

WINS – Today I accomplished or was successful at:

_____
_____
_____
_____
_____

Daily Reflection

Week 3 Reflection – Looking Back

Take time to reflect on the previous week

GENERAL REFLECTION:
How am I feeling overall about this past week?

_____

_____

_____

_____

_____

_____

CHALLENGES:
What were my greatest challenges this week?

_____

_____

_____

_____

_____

_____

ACHIEVEMENTS:
What were my greatest achievements this week?

_____

_____

_____

_____

_____

_____

Week 3 Reflection – Looking Ahead

Think about my goals and intensions for the coming week

IMPROVEMENT PLAN:

What can I do different this week to become a better person?

_____

_____

_____

_____

_____

_____

GOALS AND PLANS FOR THE COMING WEEK:

What do you want to accomplish this week?

_____

_____

_____

_____

_____

TOP PRIORITY:

What are my top priorities for the coming week?

_____

_____

_____

_____

_____

You don't fail overnight.
Instead, failure is a few errors
in judgement, repeated
every day.

-Jim Rohn-

Week 4

Journaling

Date: ___ / ___ / _____   M T W TH F S SU

Gratitude - Today I am grateful for:

_____

_____

_____

_____

_____

Remember – A good memory I will cherish from today is:

_____

_____

_____

_____

_____

Opportunities To Learn - Today I learned that:

_____

_____

_____

_____

_____

Wins – Today I accomplished or was successful at:

_____

_____

_____

_____

_____

Daily Reflection

59

Date: ___ / ___ / ___   M T W TH F S SU

GRATITUDE - Today I am grateful for:

_____
_____
_____
_____
_____

REMEMBER – A good memory I will cherish from today is:

_____
_____
_____
_____
_____

OPPORTUNITIES TO LEARN - Today I learned that:

_____
_____
_____
_____
_____

WINS – Today I accomplished or was successful at:

_____
_____
_____
_____
_____

Daily Reflection

Date: ____/____/____   M T W TH F S SU

GRATITUDE - Today I am grateful for:

_____
_____
_____
_____
_____

REMEMBER – A good memory I will cherish from today is:

_____
_____
_____
_____
_____

OPPORTUNITIES TO LEARN - Today I learned that:

_____
_____
_____
_____
_____

WINS – Today I accomplished or was successful at:

_____
_____
_____
_____
_____

Daily Reflection

Date: ____ / ____ / ____   M T W TH F S SU

GRATITUDE - Today I am grateful for:

_____

_____

_____

_____

_____

REMEMBER – A good memory I will cherish from today is:

_____

_____

_____

_____

_____

OPPORTUNITIES TO LEARN - Today I learned that:

_____

_____

_____

_____

_____

WINS – Today I accomplished or was successful at:

_____

_____

_____

_____

_____

Daily Reflection

Date: ___/___/_____   M T W TH F S SU

GRATITUDE - Today I am grateful for:

_____
_____
_____
_____
_____

REMEMBER – A good memory I will cherish from today is:

_____
_____
_____
_____
_____

OPPORTUNITIES TO LEARN - Today I learned that:

_____
_____
_____
_____
_____

WINS – Today I accomplished or was successful at:

_____
_____
_____
_____
_____

Daily Reflection

Date: ___ / ___ / _____   M T W TH F S SU

GRATITUDE - Today I am grateful for:

_____

_____

_____

_____

_____

REMEMBER – A good memory I will cherish from today is:

_____

_____

_____

_____

_____

OPPORTUNITIES **T**O **L**EARN - Today I learned that:

_____

_____

_____

_____

_____

WINS – Today I accomplished or was successful at:

_____

_____

_____

_____

_____

Daily Reflection

Date: ___ / ___ / ___   M T W TH F S SU

GRATITUDE - Today I am grateful for:

_____

_____

_____

_____

_____

REMEMBER – A good memory I will cherish from today is:

_____

_____

_____

_____

_____

OPPORTUNITIES TO LEARN - Today I learned that:

_____

_____

_____

_____

_____

WINS – Today I accomplished or was successful at:

_____

_____

_____

_____

_____

Week 4 Reflection – Looking Back

Take time to reflect on the previous week

GENERAL REFLECTION:

How am I feeling overall about this past week?

_____

_____

_____

_____

_____

_____

CHALLENGES:

What were my greatest challenges this week?

_____

_____

_____

_____

_____

ACHIEVEMENTS:

What were my greatest achievements this week?

_____

_____

_____

_____

_____

Week 4 Reflection – Looking Ahead

Think about my goals and intensions for the coming week

IMPROVEMENT PLAN:

What can I do different this week to become a better person?

_____
_____
_____
_____
_____
_____

GOALS AND PLANS FOR THE COMING WEEK:

What do you want to accomplish this week?

_____
_____
_____
_____
_____

TOP PRIORITY:

What are my top priorities for the coming week?

_____
_____
_____
_____
_____

The ultimate reason for setting goals is to entice you to become the person it takes to achieve them.

-Jim Rohn-

4-Week Review And Insights

Review and reflect on the past 4 weeks

What goals and successes did I achieve the past 4 weeks?

_____

_____

_____

_____

_____

What challenges did I face in achieving my goals?

_____

_____

_____

_____

_____

What can I do to overcome these challenges in the next 4 weeks?

_____

_____

_____

_____

_____

Additional insights and reflections from the past 4 weeks:

_____

_____

_____

_____

_____

Looking Ahead To The Next 4 Weeks

Think about and write down your goals for the coming weeks

What do I want to achieve in the next 4 weeks?

_____

_____

_____

_____

What do I need to accomplish each week to achieve these goals?

Week 5: _____

_____

Week 6: _____

_____

Week 7: _____

_____

Week 8: _____

_____

What habits do I need to develop or reinforce?

_____   _____

_____   _____

_____   _____

What habits must I remove and replace with the above habits?

_____   _____

_____   _____

_____   _____

If you go to work on your plan,
your plan will go to work on you.
Whatever good things we build,
end up building us.

-Jim Rohn-

Week 5

Journaling

Date: ___ / ___ / _____   M T W TH F S SU

GRATITUDE - Today I am grateful for:

_____

_____

_____

_____

_____

REMEMBER – A good memory I will cherish from today is:

_____

_____

_____

_____

_____

OPPORTUNITIES **T**O **L**EARN - Today I learned that:

_____

_____

_____

_____

_____

WINS – Today I accomplished or was successful at:

_____

_____

_____

_____

_____

Daily Reflection

Date: ___/___/_____   M T W TH F S SU

GRATITUDE - Today I am grateful for:

_____
_____
_____
_____
_____

REMEMBER – A good memory I will cherish from today is:

_____
_____
_____
_____
_____

OPPORTUNITIES TO LEARN - Today I learned that:

_____
_____
_____
_____
_____

WINS – Today I accomplished or was successful at:

_____
_____
_____
_____
_____

Daily Reflection

Date: ____ / ___ / _____   M T W TH F S SU

GRATITUDE - Today I am grateful for:

_____
_____
_____
_____
_____

REMEMBER – A good memory I will cherish from today is:

_____
_____
_____
_____
_____

OPPORTUNITIES **T**O **L**EARN - Today I learned that:

_____
_____
_____
_____
_____

WINS – Today I accomplished or was successful at:

_____
_____
_____
_____
_____

Daily Reflection

Date: ___/___/____   M T W TH F S SU

GRATITUDE - Today I am grateful for:

_____

_____

_____

_____

_____

REMEMBER – A good memory I will cherish from today is:

_____

_____

_____

_____

_____

OPPORTUNITIES TO LEARN - Today I learned that:

_____

_____

_____

_____

_____

WINS – Today I accomplished or was successful at:

_____

_____

_____

_____

_____

Daily Reflection

Date: ___/___/___   M T W TH F S SU

GRATITUDE - Today I am grateful for:

_____
_____
_____
_____
_____

REMEMBER – A good memory I will cherish from today is:

_____
_____
_____
_____
_____

OPPORTUNITIES **T**O **L**EARN - Today I learned that:

_____
_____
_____
_____
_____

WINS – Today I accomplished or was successful at:

_____
_____
_____
_____
_____

Daily Reflection

Date: ____ / ____ / _____   M T W TH F S SU

GRATITUDE - Today I am grateful for:

_____
_____
_____
_____
_____

REMEMBER – A good memory I will cherish from today is:

_____
_____
_____
_____
_____

OPPORTUNITIES TO LEARN - Today I learned that:

_____
_____
_____
_____
_____

WINS – Today I accomplished or was successful at:

_____
_____
_____
_____
_____

Daily Reflection

Date: ___ / ___ / _____   M T W TH F S SU

GRATITUDE - Today I am grateful for:

_____

_____

_____

_____

_____

REMEMBER – A good memory I will cherish from today is:

_____

_____

_____

_____

_____

OPPORTUNITIES **T**O **L**EARN - Today I learned that:

_____

_____

_____

_____

_____

WINS – Today I accomplished or was successful at:

_____

_____

_____

_____

_____

Daily Reflection

Week 5 Reflection – Looking Back

Take time to reflect on the previous week

GENERAL REFLECTION:

How am I feeling overall about this past week?

_____

_____

_____

_____

_____

_____

CHALLENGES:

What were my greatest challenges this week?

_____

_____

_____

_____

_____

_____

ACHIEVEMENTS:

What were my greatest achievements this week?

_____

_____

_____

_____

_____

_____

Week 5 Reflection – Looking Ahead

Think about my goals and intensions for the coming week

IMPROVEMENT PLAN:
What can I do different this week to become a better person?

_____

_____

_____

_____

_____

_____

GOALS AND PLANS FOR THE COMING WEEK:
What do you want to accomplish this week?

_____

_____

_____

_____

_____

TOP PRIORITY:
What are my top priorities for the coming week?

_____

_____

_____

_____

_____

You cannot believe what it does to the human spirit to maximize your human potential and stretch yourself to the limit.

-Jim Rohn-

Week 6

Journaling

Date: ___ / ___ / _____   M T W TH F S SU

GRATITUDE - Today I am grateful for:

_____
_____
_____
_____
_____

REMEMBER – A good memory I will cherish from today is:

_____
_____
_____
_____
_____

OPPORTUNITIES **T**O **L**EARN - Today I learned that:

_____
_____
_____
_____
_____

WINS – Today I accomplished or was successful at:

_____
_____
_____
_____
_____

Daily Reflection

Date: ___/___/_____   M T W TH F S SU

GRATITUDE - Today I am grateful for:

_____
_____
_____
_____
_____

REMEMBER – A good memory I will cherish from today is:

_____
_____
_____
_____
_____

OPPORTUNITIES TO LEARN - Today I learned that:

_____
_____
_____
_____
_____

WINS – Today I accomplished or was successful at:

_____
_____
_____
_____
_____

Daily Reflection

Date: ___/___/___   M T W TH F S SU

GRATITUDE - Today I am grateful for:

_____
_____
_____
_____
_____

REMEMBER – A good memory I will cherish from today is:

_____
_____
_____
_____
_____

OPPORTUNITIES TO LEARN - Today I learned that:

_____
_____
_____
_____
_____

WINS – Today I accomplished or was successful at:

_____
_____
_____
_____
_____

Daily Reflection

Date: ___/___/_____   M T W TH F S SU

GRATITUDE - Today I am grateful for:

_____
_____
_____
_____
_____

REMEMBER – A good memory I will cherish from today is:

_____
_____
_____
_____
_____

OPPORTUNITIES **T**O **L**EARN - Today I learned that:

_____
_____
_____
_____
_____

WINS – Today I accomplished or was successful at:

_____
_____
_____
_____
_____

Daily Reflection

Date: ___ / ___ / _____   M T W TH F S SU

GRATITUDE - Today I am grateful for:

_____
_____
_____
_____
_____

REMEMBER – A good memory I will cherish from today is:

_____
_____
_____
_____
_____

OPPORTUNITIES **T**O **L**EARN - Today I learned that:

_____
_____
_____
_____
_____

WINS – Today I accomplished or was successful at:

_____
_____
_____
_____
_____

Daily Reflection

Date: ___/___/_____   M T W TH F S SU

GRATITUDE - Today I am grateful for:

_____
_____
_____
_____
_____

REMEMBER – A good memory I will cherish from today is:

_____
_____
_____
_____
_____

OPPORTUNITIES **T**O **L**EARN - Today I learned that:

_____
_____
_____
_____
_____

WINS – Today I accomplished or was successful at:

_____
_____
_____
_____
_____

Daily Reflection

Date: ___ / ___ / ___   M T W TH F S SU

GRATITUDE - Today I am grateful for:

_____
_____
_____
_____
_____

REMEMBER – A good memory I will cherish from today is:

_____
_____
_____
_____
_____

OPPORTUNITIES **T**O **L**EARN - Today I learned that:

_____
_____
_____
_____
_____

WINS – Today I accomplished or was successful at:

_____
_____
_____
_____
_____

Daily Reflection

Week 6 Reflection – Looking Back

Take time to reflect on the previous week

GENERAL REFLECTION:

How am I feeling overall about this past week?

_____

_____

_____

_____

_____

_____

CHALLENGES:

What were my greatest challenges this week?

_____

_____

_____

_____

_____

_____

ACHIEVEMENTS:

What were my greatest achievements this week?

_____

_____

_____

_____

_____

_____

Week 6 Reflection – Looking Ahead

Think about my goals and intensions for the coming week

IMPROVEMENT PLAN:

What can I do different this week to become a better person?

_____

_____

_____

_____

_____

_____

GOALS AND PLANS FOR THE COMING WEEK:

What do you want to accomplish this week?

_____

_____

_____

_____

_____

_____

TOP PRIORITY:

What are my top priorities for the coming week?

_____

_____

_____

_____

_____

_____

Success is nothing more than
a few simple disciplines,
practiced every day.

-Jim Rohn-

Week 7

Journaling

Date: ___ / ___ / ___   M T W TH F S SU

GRATITUDE - Today I am grateful for:

_____
_____
_____
_____
_____

REMEMBER – A good memory I will cherish from today is:

_____
_____
_____
_____
_____

OPPORTUNITIES **T**O **L**EARN - Today I learned that:

_____
_____
_____
_____
_____

WINS – Today I accomplished or was successful at:

_____
_____
_____
_____
_____

Daily Reflection

Date: ___/___/_____   M T W TH F S SU

GRATITUDE - Today I am grateful for:

_____
_____
_____
_____
_____

REMEMBER – A good memory I will cherish from today is:

_____
_____
_____
_____
_____

OPPORTUNITIES TO LEARN - Today I learned that:

_____
_____
_____
_____
_____

WINS – Today I accomplished or was successful at:

_____
_____
_____
_____
_____

Daily Reflection

Date: ___ / ___ / _____   M T W TH F S SU

GRATITUDE - Today I am grateful for:

_____

_____

_____

_____

_____

REMEMBER – A good memory I will cherish from today is:

_____

_____

_____

_____

_____

OPPORTUNITIES **T**O **L**EARN - Today I learned that:

_____

_____

_____

_____

_____

WINS – Today I accomplished or was successful at:

_____

_____

_____

_____

_____

Daily Reflection

Date: ___/___/_____ M T W TH F S SU

GRATITUDE - Today I am grateful for:

_____
_____
_____
_____
_____

REMEMBER – A good memory I will cherish from today is:

_____
_____
_____
_____
_____

OPPORTUNITIES TO LEARN - Today I learned that:

_____
_____
_____
_____
_____

WINS – Today I accomplished or was successful at:

_____
_____
_____
_____
_____

Daily Reflection

Date: ___ / ___ / _____   M T W TH F S SU

GRATITUDE - Today I am grateful for:

_____

_____

_____

_____

_____

REMEMBER – A good memory I will cherish from today is:

_____

_____

_____

_____

_____

OPPORTUNITIES TO LEARN - Today I learned that:

_____

_____

_____

_____

_____

WINS – Today I accomplished or was successful at:

_____

_____

_____

_____

_____

Daily Reflection

Date: ___ / ___ / _____   M T W TH F S SU

GRATITUDE - Today I am grateful for:

_____
_____
_____
_____
_____

REMEMBER – A good memory I will cherish from today is:

_____
_____
_____
_____
_____

OPPORTUNITIES TO LEARN - Today I learned that:

_____
_____
_____
_____
_____

WINS – Today I accomplished or was successful at:

_____
_____
_____
_____
_____

Daily Reflection

Date: ___/___/___   M T W TH F S SU

G RATITUDE - Today I am grateful for:

_____
_____
_____
_____
_____

R EMEMBER – A good memory I will cherish from today is:

_____
_____
_____
_____
_____

O PPORTUNITIES TO LEARN - Today I learned that:

_____
_____
_____
_____
_____

W INS – Today I accomplished or was successful at:

_____
_____
_____
_____
_____

Daily Reflection

Week 7 Reflection – Looking Back

Take time to reflect on the previous week

GENERAL REFLECTION:
How am I feeling overall about this past week?

_____

_____

_____

_____

_____

_____

CHALLENGES:
What were my greatest challenges this week?

_____

_____

_____

_____

_____

_____

ACHIEVEMENTS:
What were my greatest achievements this week?

_____

_____

_____

_____

_____

_____

Week 7 Reflection – Looking Ahead

Think about my goals and intensions for the coming week

IMPROVEMENT PLAN:
What can I do different this week to become a better person?

_____
_____
_____
_____
_____
_____

GOALS AND PLANS FOR THE COMING WEEK:
What do you want to accomplish this week?

_____
_____
_____
_____
_____

TOP PRIORITY:
What are my top priorities for the coming week?

_____
_____
_____
_____
_____

Formal education will make you a living; self-education will make you a fortune.

-Jim Rohn-

Week 8

Journaling

Date: ___ / ___ / _____   M T W TH F S SU

GRATITUDE - Today I am grateful for:

_____

_____

_____

_____

_____

REMEMBER – A good memory I will cherish from today is:

_____

_____

_____

_____

_____

OPPORTUNITIES **T**O **L**EARN - Today I learned that:

_____

_____

_____

_____

_____

WINS – Today I accomplished or was successful at:

_____

_____

_____

_____

_____

Daily Reflection

Date: ___/___/_____   M T W TH F S SU

GRATITUDE - Today I am grateful for:

_____
_____
_____
_____
_____

REMEMBER – A good memory I will cherish from today is:

_____
_____
_____
_____
_____

OPPORTUNITIES TO LEARN - Today I learned that:

_____
_____
_____
_____
_____

WINS – Today I accomplished or was successful at:

_____
_____
_____
_____
_____

Daily Reflection

Date: ___ / ___ / ___   M T W TH F S SU

GRATITUDE - Today I am grateful for:

_____

_____

_____

_____

_____

REMEMBER – A good memory I will cherish from today is:

_____

_____

_____

_____

_____

OPPORTUNITIES TO LEARN - Today I learned that:

_____

_____

_____

_____

_____

WINS – Today I accomplished or was successful at:

_____

_____

_____

_____

_____

Daily Reflection

Date: ___ / ___ / _____   M T W TH F S SU

GRATITUDE - Today I am grateful for:

_____
_____
_____
_____
_____

REMEMBER – A good memory I will cherish from today is:

_____
_____
_____
_____
_____

OPPORTUNITIES **T**O **L**EARN - Today I learned that:

_____
_____
_____
_____
_____

WINS – Today I accomplished or was successful at:

_____
_____
_____
_____
_____

Daily Reflection

Date: ____ / ____ / _____   M T W TH F S SU

GRATITUDE - Today I am grateful for:

_____
_____
_____
_____
_____

REMEMBER – A good memory I will cherish from today is:

_____
_____
_____
_____
_____

OPPORTUNITIES TO LEARN - Today I learned that:

_____
_____
_____
_____
_____

WINS – Today I accomplished or was successful at:

_____
_____
_____
_____
_____

Daily Reflection

Date: ___/___/___   M T W TH F S SU

GRATITUDE - Today I am grateful for:

_____

_____

_____

_____

_____

REMEMBER – A good memory I will cherish from today is:

_____

_____

_____

_____

_____

OPPORTUNITIES **T**O **L**EARN - Today I learned that:

_____

_____

_____

_____

_____

WINS – Today I accomplished or was successful at:

_____

_____

_____

_____

_____

Daily Reflection

Date: ___ / ___ / _____   M T W TH F S SU

GRATITUDE - Today I am grateful for:

_____
_____
_____
_____
_____

REMEMBER – A good memory I will cherish from today is:

_____
_____
_____
_____
_____

OPPORTUNITIES TO LEARN - Today I learned that:

_____
_____
_____
_____
_____

WINS – Today I accomplished or was successful at:

_____
_____
_____
_____
_____

Daily Reflection

Week 8 Reflection – Looking Back

Take time to reflect on the previous week

GENERAL REFLECTION:

How am I feeling overall about this past week?

_____

_____

_____

_____

_____

_____

CHALLENGES:

What were my greatest challenges this week?

_____

_____

_____

_____

_____

ACHIEVEMENTS:

What were my greatest achievements this week?

_____

_____

_____

_____

_____

Week 8 Reflection – Looking Ahead

Think about my goals and intensions for the coming week

IMPROVEMENT PLAN:
What can I do different this week to become a better person?

_____

_____

_____

_____

_____

_____

GOALS AND PLANS FOR THE COMING WEEK:
What do you want to accomplish this week?

_____

_____

_____

_____

_____

TOP PRIORITY:
What are my top priorities for the coming week?

_____

_____

_____

_____

_____

You cannot change your destination overnight, but you can change your direction overnight.

-Jim Rohn-

4-Week Review And Insights
Review and reflect on the past 4 weeks

What goals and successes did I achieve the past 4 weeks?

_____

_____

_____

_____

_____

What challenges did I face in achieving my goals?

_____

_____

_____

_____

_____

What can I do to overcome these challenges in the next 4 weeks?

_____

_____

_____

_____

_____

Additional insights and reflections from the past 4 weeks:

_____

_____

_____

_____

_____

Looking Ahead To The Next 4 Weeks

Think about and write down your goals for the coming weeks

What do I want to achieve in the next 4 weeks?

_____

_____

_____

_____

What do I need to accomplish each week to achieve these goals?

Week 9: _____

_____

Week 10: _____

_____

Week 11: _____

_____

Week 12: _____

_____

What habits do I need to develop or reinforce?

_____   _____

_____   _____

_____   _____

What habits must I remove and replace with the above habits?

_____   _____

_____   _____

_____   _____

Don't let your learning lead to knowledge. Let your learning lead to action.

-Jim Rohn-

Week 9

Journaling

Date: ___ / ___ / ___   M T W TH F S SU

GRATITUDE - Today I am grateful for:

_____

_____

_____

_____

_____

REMEMBER – A good memory I will cherish from today is:

_____

_____

_____

_____

_____

OPPORTUNITIES TO LEARN - Today I learned that:

_____

_____

_____

_____

_____

WINS – Today I accomplished or was successful at:

_____

_____

_____

_____

_____

Daily Reflection

Date: ___ / ___ / ___   M T W TH F S SU

GRATITUDE - Today I am grateful for:

_____
_____
_____
_____
_____

REMEMBER – A good memory I will cherish from today is:

_____
_____
_____
_____
_____

OPPORTUNITIES TO LEARN - Today I learned that:

_____
_____
_____
_____
_____

WINS – Today I accomplished or was successful at:

_____
_____
_____
_____
_____

Daily Reflection

Date: ___ / ___ / ___   M T W TH F S SU

GRATITUDE - Today I am grateful for:

_____

_____

_____

_____

_____

REMEMBER – A good memory I will cherish from today is:

_____

_____

_____

_____

_____

OPPORTUNITIES TO LEARN - Today I learned that:

_____

_____

_____

_____

_____

WINS – Today I accomplished or was successful at:

_____

_____

_____

_____

_____

Daily Reflection

Date: ___ / ___ / _____   M T W TH F S SU

GRATITUDE - Today I am grateful for:

_____
_____
_____
_____
_____

REMEMBER – A good memory I will cherish from today is:

_____
_____
_____
_____
_____

OPPORTUNITIES TO LEARN - Today I learned that:

_____
_____
_____
_____
_____

WINS – Today I accomplished or was successful at:

_____
_____
_____
_____
_____

Daily Reflection

Date: ___ / ___ / ___   M T W TH F S SU

GRATITUDE - Today I am grateful for:

_____
_____
_____
_____
_____

REMEMBER – A good memory I will cherish from today is:

_____
_____
_____
_____
_____

OPPORTUNITIES TO LEARN - Today I learned that:

_____
_____
_____
_____
_____

WINS – Today I accomplished or was successful at:

_____
_____
_____
_____
_____

Daily Reflection

Date: ___ / ___ / ___   M T W TH F S SU

GRATITUDE - Today I am grateful for:

_____
_____
_____
_____
_____

REMEMBER – A good memory I will cherish from today is:

_____
_____
_____
_____
_____

OPPORTUNITIES TO LEARN - Today I learned that:

_____
_____
_____
_____
_____

WINS – Today I accomplished or was successful at:

_____
_____
_____
_____
_____

Daily Reflection

Date: ___/___/___   M T W TH F S SU

GRATITUDE - Today I am grateful for:

_____
_____
_____
_____
_____

REMEMBER – A good memory I will cherish from today is:

_____
_____
_____
_____
_____

OPPORTUNITIES TO LEARN - Today I learned that:

_____
_____
_____
_____
_____

WINS – Today I accomplished or was successful at:

_____
_____
_____
_____
_____

Daily Reflection

Week 9 Reflection – Looking Back

Take time to reflect on the previous week

GENERAL REFLECTION:
How am I feeling overall about this past week?

_____
_____
_____
_____
_____
_____

CHALLENGES:
What were my greatest challenges this week?

_____
_____
_____
_____
_____

ACHIEVEMENTS:
What were my greatest achievements this week?

_____
_____
_____
_____
_____

Week 9 Reflection – Looking Ahead

Think about my goals and intensions for the coming week

IMPROVEMENT PLAN:
What can I do different this week to become a better person?

_____

_____

_____

_____

_____

_____

GOALS AND PLANS FOR THE COMING WEEK:
What do you want to accomplish this week?

_____

_____

_____

_____

_____

_____

TOP PRIORITY:
What are my top priorities for the coming week?

_____

_____

_____

_____

_____

_____

Don't wish it was easier,
wish you were better.

-Jim Rohn-

Week 10

Journaling

Date: ___ / ___ / _____   M T W TH F S SU

GRATITUDE - Today I am grateful for:

_____
_____
_____
_____
_____

REMEMBER – A good memory I will cherish from today is:

_____
_____
_____
_____
_____

OPPORTUNITIES TO LEARN - Today I learned that:

_____
_____
_____
_____
_____

WINS – Today I accomplished or was successful at:

_____
_____
_____
_____
_____

Daily Reflection

Date: ___/___/_____   M T W TH F S SU

GRATITUDE - Today I am grateful for:

_____
_____
_____
_____
_____

REMEMBER – A good memory I will cherish from today is:

_____
_____
_____
_____
_____

OPPORTUNITIES TO LEARN - Today I learned that:

_____
_____
_____
_____
_____

WINS – Today I accomplished or was successful at:

_____
_____
_____
_____
_____

Daily Reflection

Date: ___ / ___ / _____   M T W TH F S SU

GRATITUDE - Today I am grateful for:

_____

_____

_____

_____

_____

REMEMBER – A good memory I will cherish from today is:

_____

_____

_____

_____

_____

OPPORTUNITIES TO LEARN - Today I learned that:

_____

_____

_____

_____

_____

WINS – Today I accomplished or was successful at:

_____

_____

_____

_____

_____

Daily Reflection

Date: ___ / ___ / ___   **M T W TH F S SU**

Gratitude - Today I am grateful for:

_____

_____

_____

_____

_____

Remember – A good memory I will cherish from today is:

_____

_____

_____

_____

_____

Opportunities To Learn - Today I learned that:

_____

_____

_____

_____

_____

Wins – Today I accomplished or was successful at:

_____

_____

_____

_____

_____

Daily Reflection

Date: ___ / ___ / ___   M T W TH F S SU

GRATITUDE - Today I am grateful for:

_____
_____
_____
_____
_____

REMEMBER – A good memory I will cherish from today is:

_____
_____
_____
_____
_____

OPPORTUNITIES **T**O **L**EARN - Today I learned that:

_____
_____
_____
_____
_____

WINS – Today I accomplished or was successful at:

_____
_____
_____
_____
_____

Daily Reflection

Date: ___/___/___   M T W TH F S SU

GRATITUDE - Today I am grateful for:

_____
_____
_____
_____
_____

REMEMBER – A good memory I will cherish from today is:

_____
_____
_____
_____
_____

OPPORTUNITIES TO LEARN - Today I learned that:

_____
_____
_____
_____
_____

WINS – Today I accomplished or was successful at:

_____
_____
_____
_____
_____

Daily Reflection

Date: ___/___/___   M T W TH F S SU

GRATITUDE - Today I am grateful for:

_____
_____
_____
_____
_____

REMEMBER – A good memory I will cherish from today is:

_____
_____
_____
_____
_____

OPPORTUNITIES TO LEARN - Today I learned that:

_____
_____
_____
_____
_____

WINS – Today I accomplished or was successful at:

_____
_____
_____
_____
_____

Daily Reflection

Week 10 Reflection – Looking Back

Take time to reflect on the previous week

GENERAL REFLECTION:
How am I feeling overall about this past week?

_____

_____

_____

_____

_____

_____

CHALLENGES:
What were my greatest challenges this week?

_____

_____

_____

_____

_____

_____

ACHIEVEMENTS:
What were my greatest achievements this week?

_____

_____

_____

_____

_____

_____

Week 10 Reflection – Looking Ahead

Think about my goals and intensions for the coming week

IMPROVEMENT PLAN:
What can I do different this week to become a better person?

_____
_____
_____
_____
_____
_____

GOALS AND PLANS FOR THE COMING WEEK:
What do you want to accomplish this week?

_____
_____
_____
_____
_____

TOP PRIORITY:
What are my top priorities for the coming week?

_____
_____
_____
_____
_____

*We must all suffer one
of two pains: the pain of
discipline or the pain of regret.*

-Jim Rohn-

Week 11

Journaling

Date: ___ / ___ / ___   M T W TH F S SU

GRATITUDE - Today I am grateful for:

_____
_____
_____
_____
_____

REMEMBER – A good memory I will cherish from today is:

_____
_____
_____
_____
_____

OPPORTUNITIES TO LEARN - Today I learned that:

_____
_____
_____
_____
_____

WINS – Today I accomplished or was successful at:

_____
_____
_____
_____
_____

Daily Reflection

Date: ___ / ___ / ___   M T W TH F S SU

GRATITUDE - Today I am grateful for:

_____

_____

_____

_____

_____

REMEMBER – A good memory I will cherish from today is:

_____

_____

_____

_____

_____

OPPORTUNITIES **T**O **L**EARN - Today I learned that:

_____

_____

_____

_____

_____

WINS – Today I accomplished or was successful at:

_____

_____

_____

_____

_____

Daily Reflection

Date: ___ / ___ / ___   M T W TH F S SU

GRATITUDE - Today I am grateful for:

_____

_____

_____

_____

_____

REMEMBER – A good memory I will cherish from today is:

_____

_____

_____

_____

_____

OPPORTUNITIES TO LEARN - Today I learned that:

_____

_____

_____

_____

_____

WINS – Today I accomplished or was successful at:

_____

_____

_____

_____

_____

Daily Reflection

Date: ___/___/___   M T W TH F S SU

GRATITUDE - Today I am grateful for:

_____
_____
_____
_____
_____

REMEMBER – A good memory I will cherish from today is:

_____
_____
_____
_____
_____

OPPORTUNITIES TO LEARN - Today I learned that:

_____
_____
_____
_____
_____

WINS – Today I accomplished or was successful at:

_____
_____
_____
_____
_____

Daily Reflection

Date: ___ / ___ / _____   M T W TH F S SU

GRATITUDE - Today I am grateful for:

_____
_____
_____
_____
_____

REMEMBER – A good memory I will cherish from today is:

_____
_____
_____
_____
_____

OPPORTUNITIES TO LEARN - Today I learned that:

_____
_____
_____
_____
_____

WINS – Today I accomplished or was successful at:

_____
_____
_____
_____
_____

Daily Reflection

Date: ___ / ___ / _____   M T W TH F S SU

GRATITUDE - Today I am grateful for:

_____
_____
_____
_____
_____

REMEMBER – A good memory I will cherish from today is:

_____
_____
_____
_____
_____

OPPORTUNITIES TO LEARN - Today I learned that:

_____
_____
_____
_____
_____

WINS – Today I accomplished or was successful at:

_____
_____
_____
_____
_____

Daily Reflection

Date: ___ / ___ / _____   M T W TH F S SU

GRATITUDE - Today I am grateful for:

_____

_____

_____

_____

_____

REMEMBER – A good memory I will cherish from today is:

_____

_____

_____

_____

_____

OPPORTUNITIES TO LEARN - Today I learned that:

_____

_____

_____

_____

_____

WINS – Today I accomplished or was successful at:

_____

_____

_____

_____

_____

Daily Reflection

Week 11 Reflection – Looking Back

Take time to reflect on the previous week

GENERAL REFLECTION:
How am I feeling overall about this past week?

_____

_____

_____

_____

_____

_____

CHALLENGES:
What were my greatest challenges this week?

_____

_____

_____

_____

_____

_____

ACHIEVEMENTS:
What were my greatest achievements this week?

_____

_____

_____

_____

_____

_____

Week 11 Reflection – Looking Ahead

Think about my goals and intensions for the coming week

IMPROVEMENT PLAN:
What can I do different this week to become a better person?

_____

_____

_____

_____

_____

_____

GOALS AND PLANS FOR THE COMING WEEK:
What do you want to accomplish this week?

_____

_____

_____

_____

_____

TOP PRIORITY:
What are my top priorities for the coming week?

_____

_____

_____

_____

_____

Motivation is what gets you started. Habit is what keeps you going.

-Jim Rohn-

Week 12

Journaling

Date: ___ / ___ / _____   M T W TH F S SU

GRATITUDE - Today I am grateful for:

_____
_____
_____
_____
_____

REMEMBER – A good memory I will cherish from today is:

_____
_____
_____
_____
_____

OPPORTUNITIES TO LEARN - Today I learned that:

_____
_____
_____
_____
_____

WINS – Today I accomplished or was successful at:

_____
_____
_____
_____
_____

Daily Reflection

Date: ____ / ____ / ____   M T W TH F S SU

GRATITUDE - Today I am grateful for:

_____

_____

_____

_____

_____

REMEMBER – A good memory I will cherish from today is:

_____

_____

_____

_____

_____

OPPORTUNITIES TO LEARN - Today I learned that:

_____

_____

_____

_____

_____

WINS – Today I accomplished or was successful at:

_____

_____

_____

_____

_____

Daily Reflection

Date: ___ / ___ / _____   M T W TH F S SU

GRATITUDE - Today I am grateful for:

_____

_____

_____

_____

_____

REMEMBER – A good memory I will cherish from today is:

_____

_____

_____

_____

_____

OPPORTUNITIES TO LEARN - Today I learned that:

_____

_____

_____

_____

_____

WINS – Today I accomplished or was successful at:

_____

_____

_____

_____

_____

Daily Reflection

Date: ___ / ___ / _____   M T W TH F S SU

GRATITUDE - Today I am grateful for:

_____
_____
_____
_____
_____

REMEMBER – A good memory I will cherish from today is:

_____
_____
_____
_____
_____

OPPORTUNITIES TO LEARN - Today I learned that:

_____
_____
_____
_____
_____

WINS – Today I accomplished or was successful at:

_____
_____
_____
_____
_____

Daily Reflection

Date: ___/___/_____   **M T W TH F S SU**

GRATITUDE - Today I am grateful for:

_____

_____

_____

_____

_____

REMEMBER – A good memory I will cherish from today is:

_____

_____

_____

_____

_____

OPPORTUNITIES TO LEARN - Today I learned that:

_____

_____

_____

_____

_____

WINS – Today I accomplished or was successful at:

_____

_____

_____

_____

_____

Daily Reflection

Date: ___/___/_____   M T W TH F S SU

GRATITUDE - Today I am grateful for:

_____

_____

_____

_____

_____

REMEMBER – A good memory I will cherish from today is:

_____

_____

_____

_____

_____

OPPORTUNITIES TO LEARN - Today I learned that:

_____

_____

_____

_____

_____

WINS – Today I accomplished or was successful at:

_____

_____

_____

_____

_____

Daily Reflection

Date: ___/___/___   M T W TH F S SU

GRATITUDE - Today I am grateful for:

_____
_____
_____
_____
_____

REMEMBER – A good memory I will cherish from today is:

_____
_____
_____
_____
_____

OPPORTUNITIES TO LEARN - Today I learned that:

_____
_____
_____
_____
_____

WINS – Today I accomplished or was successful at:

_____
_____
_____
_____
_____

Daily Reflection

Week 12 Reflection – Looking Back

Take time to reflect on the previous week

GENERAL REFLECTION:
How am I feeling overall about this past week?

_____

_____

_____

_____

_____

_____

CHALLENGES:
What were my greatest challenges this week?

_____

_____

_____

_____

_____

ACHIEVEMENTS:
What were my greatest achievements this week?

_____

_____

_____

_____

_____

Week 12 Reflection – Looking Ahead

Think about my goals and intensions for the coming week

IMPROVEMENT PLAN:
What can I do different this week to become a better person?

_____

_____

_____

_____

_____

_____

GOALS AND PLANS FOR THE COMING WEEK:
What do you want to accomplish this week?

_____

_____

_____

_____

_____

TOP PRIORITY:
What are my top priorities for the coming week?

_____

_____

_____

_____

_____

_____

The big challenge is to become all that you have the possibility of becoming.

-Jim Rohn-

4-Week Review And Insights

Review and reflect on the past 4 weeks

What goals and successes did I achieve the past 4 weeks?

_____

_____

_____

_____

_____

What challenges did I face in achieving my goals?

_____

_____

_____

_____

_____

What can I do to overcome these challenges in the next 4 weeks?

_____

_____

_____

_____

_____

Additional insights and reflections from the past 4 weeks:

_____

_____

_____

_____

_____

Looking Ahead To The Next 4 Weeks

Think about and write down your goals for the coming weeks.

What do I want to achieve in the next 4 weeks?

_____

_____

_____

_____

What do I need to accomplish each week to achieve these goals?

Week 13: _____

_____

Week 14: _____

_____

Week 15: _____

_____

Week 16: _____

_____

What habits do I need to develop or reinforce?

_____   _____

_____   _____

_____   _____

What habits must I remove and replace with the above habits?

_____   _____

_____   _____

_____   _____

Notes

Notes

Notes

Notes

Notes

PLE PUBLISHING & PROMOTIONS

Printed in Great Britain
by Amazon